STUDY GUIDE

YOUR
PERSONAL
GUIDE TO
LEADERSHIP
LONGEVITY

LEADERFIT

Copyright © 2021 by Andrew Momon, Jr.

Published by AVAIL.

All rights reserved. No portion of this book may be reproduced, stored in a retrieval system, or transmitted in any form or by any means—electronic, mechanical, photocopy, recording, scanning, or other—except for brief quotations in critical reviews or articles, without prior written permission of the author.

Scripture quotations marked NIV are taken from the Holy Bible, New International Version®, NIV®. Copyright © 1973, 1978, 1984, 2011 by Biblica, Inc.™ Used by permission of Zondervan. All rights reserved worldwide. www.zondervan.com. The "NIV" and "New International Version" are trademarks registered in the United States Patent and Trademark Office by Biblica, Inc.™

For foreign and subsidiary rights, contact the author.

Cover design by: Joe De Leon
Photography by: Andrew van Tilborgh

ISBN: 978-1-954089-28-0   1 2 3 4 5 6 7 8 9 10

Printed in the United States of America

STUDY GUIDE

YOUR
PERSONAL
GUIDE TO
LEADERSHIP
LONGEVITY

LEADERFIT

ANDREW MOMON JR.

CONTENTS

Chapter 1. Introduction 6

Chapter 2. Leader Fitness As a Mindset 14

Chapter 3. Fit to Lead 22

Chapter 4. Discipline Is My Superpower 30

Chapter 5. How's Your Core Strength? (Core Values) 36

Chapter 6. The Strong Survive 44

Chapter 7. Muscle Memory 52

Chapter 8. Follow the Leader: Are You Leading Others to Life or Death? 60

Chapter 9. Emotional Fitness 68

Chapter 10. Family Fitness 76

Chapter 11. LeaderFit Unleashed 84

INTRODUCTION

*May our footprints not only take us to our destiny,
but may they also forge a trail for others to follow.*

READING TIME

As you read the "Introduction" in *LeaderFit*, review, reflect on, and respond to the text by answering the following questions.

REVIEW, REFLECT, AND RESPOND:

How has leadership, good or bad, impacted you and shaped the person you have become?

_____
_____
_____
_____
_____
_____
_____
_____
_____

How would you describe your personal leadership style or philosophy?

_____
_____
_____
_____
_____
_____
_____
_____
_____
_____
_____
_____

What correlation could you derive between physical fitness and leadership?

___

Consider leaders you have observed in the past who start well, yet do not finish the course or excel to elite levels. What are the factors that inhibited their growth? Can you make the same observations about your own leadership journey?

___

What changes about your perception of leadership when you consider it as a process rather than a destination?

_____
_____
_____
_____
_____
_____
_____

What forward steps have you had to take in spite of the uncertainties of the future?

_____
_____
_____
_____
_____
_____
_____

As of this moment, how would you rate your degree of LeaderFitness? What commitments are you willing to make as you launch towards the next phase of your LeaderFit potential?

_____
_____
_____
_____
_____
_____
_____

> **REFLECT ON**
>
> *LeaderFit is defined as, "the conditioned ability to positively influence, motivate, equip, and empower others to the achievement of a goal or outcome over a sustained period of time with sustaining impact."*

Consider the statement above, and answer the following questions:

Conditioning is usually associated with training and fitness. What type of training, physical or otherwise have you engaged in?

_____
_____
_____
_____
_____
_____
_____
_____

What are effective ways you have seen others be motivated or positively influenced?

_____
_____
_____
_____
_____
_____
_____
_____

How do you factor sustainability into your own leadership pursuits?

_____
_____
_____
_____
_____
_____
_____
_____

CHAPTER 1

LEADER FITNESS AS A MINDSET

I am equipped, suitable, and prepared to accomplish my goals for today. I carry within me the ability to be productive, and my productivity will influence those I encounter.

READING TIME

As you read Chapter 1: "LeaderFitness As a Mindset" in *LeaderFit*, review, reflect on, and respond to the text by answering the following questions.

REVIEW, REFLECT, AND RESPOND:

What are typical goals people set from year to year? What goals have you found yourself setting on a semi-annual basis?

_____
_____
_____
_____
_____

Can you identify the fallacy in traditional self-help "think yourself successful" strategies? If you've employed these in your own life, are you pleased or wish to see improvements in the outcomes?

_____
_____
_____
_____

When you consider the steps necessary for you to become LeaderFit, are these primarily in the arena of physical fitness or in other segments of your life? What are some other questions you could ask yourself to establish a baseline for which to begin your LeaderFit journey?

_____
_____
_____
_____

Who are some influential leaders you admire? When you consider the attributes that qualify them as "successful" in your perspective, are you drawn more to their capacity to lead people towards a common goal or their strategic thinking and cognitive disciplines?

_____
_____
_____
_____
_____
_____

What research have you undergone, or could you undertake, to better understand what is behind the successful tenure of elite leaders and performers whom you would like to emulate?

_____
_____
_____
_____
_____
_____

If the pursuit of LeaderFitness is truly a journey and the adoption of a lifestyle, what are small steps you can begin to take today towards your future?

_____
_____
_____
_____
_____
_____

What tools are you lacking to attain your goals in leadership and fitness? Do you know how to ascertain the resources you will need?

_____
_____
_____
_____
_____
_____
_____
_____

What is your current level of discipline, endurance, focus, and commitment to seeing your goals through to completion?

_____
_____
_____
_____
_____
_____
_____
_____

What are sources of inspiration you can turn to when you feel your motivation towards personal development waning?

_____
_____
_____
_____
_____
_____
_____
_____

> **REFLECT ON**
>
> *Because of the Lord's great love we are not consumed, for his compassions never fail. They are new every morning; great is your faithfulness.*
>
> —*Lamentations 3:22-23 (NIV)*

Consider Lamentations 3:22-23, and answer the following questions:

How can you begin to incorporate the idea of new possibilities and new beginnings each day into your life?

_____
_____
_____
_____
_____
_____
_____
_____

How do you discern God's love and compassion in your personal life?

_____
_____
_____
_____
_____
_____
_____
_____

How would you encourage someone who is discouraged and unable to find hope in each new day?

___

___

___

___

___

___

___

___

___

CHAPTER 2

FIT TO LEAD

The call of leadership is a vocation of unrelenting persistence, but we must lead. We must lead with the humility that is appropriate to impact change on the environment around us based on the inner conviction of discontent for the status quo.

READING TIME

As you read Chapter 2: "Fit to Lead" in *LeaderFit*, review, reflect on, and respond to the text by answering the following questions.

REVIEW, REFLECT, AND RESPOND:

Why do you think people are so quick to judge others in leadership positions regardless of their personal qualifications or expertise?

_____
_____
_____
_____
_____
_____
_____
_____
_____

If you have been entrusted as an "established leader," was the level of responsibility equivalent to your expectations, or did you find yourself overwhelmed?

_____
_____
_____
_____
_____
_____
_____
_____
_____
_____

What does clarity look like in your mind?

_____
_____
_____
_____
_____

What have you found that gives you the most clarity when your way appears dimly lit or the path is ambiguous?

_____
_____
_____
_____
_____

What are four things effective leadership and physical fitness both require?

1) _____
2) _____
3) _____
4) _____

Have you fully and honestly assessed the cost of leadership? What are you prepared to sacrifice to answer the responsibility and call of leadership?

_____
_____
_____
_____
_____

What are ways you can assess your fortitude for the journey and commitment of leadership?

_____
_____
_____
_____
_____

Andrew's commitment to fitness is reflected in multiple assets of life: physical, spiritual, emotional, relational, and intellectual. How do you rank your current level of LeaderFitness in these arenas?

_____
_____
_____
_____
_____
_____
_____
_____

Just as our physical health standards and requirements vary in different seasons of life, so too do different seasons of leadership require different responses. Are your current habits and disciplines appropriate for the season of leadership in which you reside?

_____
_____
_____
_____
_____

> **REFLECT ON**
>
> *Life's most persistent and urgent question: What are you doing for others?"*
>
> —*Martin Luther King, Jr.*

Consider the quote from Dr. King, and answer the following questions:

Can you identify with Dr. King's urgency when it comes to serving others? Where do you think this originates for you?

_____
_____
_____
_____
_____
_____
_____

Dr. King's call to leadership ultimately called him to sacrifice his life to be an enactor of change. What are you prepared to sacrifice for the benefit of those you serve in leadership?

_____
_____
_____
_____
_____
_____
_____
_____

CHAPTER 3

DISCIPLINE IS MY SUPERPOWER

If you want to accomplish anything significant, you must marry your desire with the discipline to carry it out. You must prescribe, predetermine, and set in place a plan of behavior that facilitates your stated desire.

READING TIME

As you read Chapter 3: "Discipline Is My Superpower" in *LeaderFit*, review, reflect on, and respond to the text by answering the following questions.

REVIEW, REFLECT, AND RESPOND:

How would you answer Andrew's question, "How much do you want what you say you want?"

_____
_____
_____
_____
_____

Are you able to correlate your pattern of success with your level of adherence to a personal code of conduct? What are your observations?

_____
_____
_____
_____
_____

Consider Andrew's example of his personal pushup challenge. How does this example help illuminate the difference between achieving an accomplishment and establishing a code of discipline over time?

_____
_____
_____
_____
_____

Consider some leaders or other elite performers who are truly extraordinary. What role does discipline play in their success? What can you learn from and apply to your life from these examples?

___

When have you and another person chosen to embark on separate journeys? What were the feelings then? How are your feelings about that separation now?

___

What is your greatest impediment when it comes to establishing a fitness regimen, or other necessary discipline in your life?

___

On page 46, the author lists the many benefits of working out that are reaped over time. Consider the discipline you wish to attain or improve, and make a similar list.

_____
_____
_____
_____
_____
_____
_____
_____
_____

How does the consideration of discipline as a responsibility rather than an attribute alter your understanding and conception of it?

_____
_____
_____
_____
_____
_____
_____
_____

What is the legacy of discipline you are building for those who come behind you?

_____
_____
_____
_____
_____
_____
_____
_____

> **REFLECT ON**
>
> *Hope deferred makes the heart sick, but a longing fulfilled is a tree of life"*
>
> —*Proverbs 13:12 (NIV)*

Consider Proverbs 13:12, and answer the following questions:

What wisdom do you see in these verses?

_____
_____
_____
_____

How does the idea that the postponement of our dreams leading to a sickened heart translate into personal motivation?

_____
_____
_____
_____

How would you feel if your dreams went unrealized? Can you imagine the joy and fulfillment of seeing them through?

_____
_____
_____
_____

CHAPTER 4

HOW'S YOUR CORE STRENGTH? (CORE VALUES)

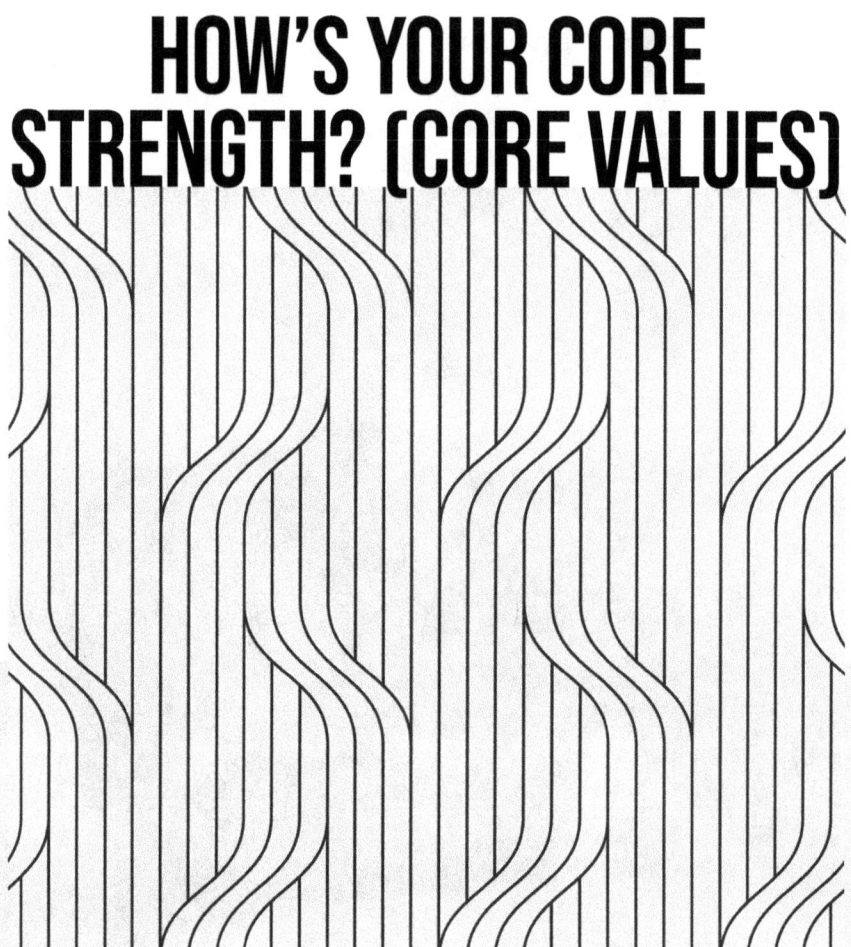

"Values are principles that guide your decisions and behaviors. When those values are good, they bring only benefits—never harm—to yourself and others."
—John C. Maxwell

READING TIME

As you read Chapter 4: "How's Your Core Strength? (Core Values)" in *LeaderFit*, review, reflect on, and respond to the text by answering the following questions.

REVIEW, REFLECT, AND RESPOND:

How consistent is the person you are when no one is looking at your public persona?

_____
_____
_____
_____
_____
_____
_____

Andrew makes the point that many will spend hours in a gym, yet their results are less than optimal because their core fundamentals and understanding of proper form and execution may be flawed. What is the correlation between a faulty core set of workout principles and faulty core values?

_____
_____
_____
_____
_____
_____
_____
_____

Consider your core values—what you value, where you spend your time, what occupies your mind and heart when you are not in public. How do these align with the image you portray or the image you wish to portray?

_____
_____
_____
_____
_____
_____
_____

Just as one's physical core is key to their overall strength and well-being, one's core values are critical to one's strength as a leader and person. How do you understand the definition of "core value"?

_____
_____
_____
_____
_____
_____
_____

Andrew suggests that we cannot strengthen that which we have not identified. What are your core values? Name at least five.

1) _____
2) _____
3) _____
4) _____
5) _____

Core exercises are vital for one's posture, overall strength, health, well-being, and prevention of injury. How might this knowledge enhance or increase your motivation to strengthen your core?

___

Andrew often tells others that he is training for life. What does that statement mean to you?

___

If you were to encounter a major obstacle tomorrow, do you feel like your commitment to your personal development would withstand the trial? What are ways in which you can begin to strengthen your resolve today?

___

Identify at least two ways you can actively build upon your core values daily.

___

> ## REFLECT ON
>
> *Run in such a way as to get the prize. Everyone who competes in the games goes into strict training. They do it to get a crown that will not last, but we do it to get a crown that will last forever. Therefore I do not run like someone running aimlessly; I do not fight like a boxer beating the air. No, I strike a blow to my body and make it my slave so that after I have preached to others, I myself will not be disqualified for the prize.*
>
> *—1 Corinthians 9:24-27 (NIV)*

Consider 1 Corinthians 9:24-27, and answer the following questions:

What role does motivation play in physical and leadership training?

_____
_____
_____
_____
_____
_____
_____

What is your personal motivation for establishing, and daily strengthening your core values?

_____
_____
_____
_____
_____
_____
_____

Paul writes that he runs, fights, and pushes so that he is worthy for the prize. What is the prize that pushes you towards the finish line?

_____
_____
_____
_____
_____

CHAPTER 5

THE STRONG SURVIVE

What are you doing today for your tomorrow? What are you preparing yourself for? If you know what you want and how to obtain it, you need preparation to attain it.

READING TIME

As you read Chapter 5: "The Strong Survive" in *LeaderFit*, review, reflect on, and respond to the text by answering the following questions

REVIEW, REFLECT, AND RESPOND:

How does the LeaderFit definition of strength expand upon conventional definitions?

_____
_____
_____
_____
_____

How do you react when you hear the phrase, "strength isn't that hard to build"? How do you differentiate "complicated" from "hard"?

_____
_____
_____
_____
_____
_____

Why are exercise selection and form so critical to a solid foundation when it comes to physical and leadership strength development?

_____
_____
_____
_____
_____
_____

How important is it to strike a balance between the principle of progressive overload and appropriate recovery time?

_____
_____
_____
_____
_____
_____

Do you tend to be led by how you feel or how you believe? What role does mental strength play in determining to which you will likely defer?

_____
_____
_____
_____
_____
_____

Andrew lists five exercises for gaining mental strength. Which of these do you currently engage in? How can you plan on adding them to a daily or weekly regime?

_____
_____
_____
_____
_____
_____

How does the notion of tolerating discomfort strike you? Why is it necessary to push the boundaries of personal comfort?

What role do interpersonal skills play in the development of interpersonal strength?

Andrew profiles his perception of a strong individual on page 73. Do you agree with his criteria? Considering these attributes and the statement "the strong survive," how would you assess your current chances of survival according to your strength level? What are ways you can improve your odds?

> **REFLECT ON**
>
> *"For our struggle is not against flesh and blood, but against the rulers, against the authorities, against the powers of this dark world and against the spiritual forces of evil in the heavenly realms"*
>
> —*Ephesians 6:12 (NIV*

Consider Ephesians 6:12, and answer the following questions:

When are you tempted to rely on your own strength as opposed to a reliance on God?

_____
_____
_____
_____
_____

What are ways you can practice dependence on God?

_____
_____
_____
_____
_____

How can you develop practices to build your spiritual strength?

_____
_____
_____
_____
_____

CHAPTER 6

MUSCLE MEMORY

In order to remain relevant and effective, you have to be a person who is committed to changing. That may sound odd, but if you are committed to change, you are committed to maintaining flexibility to relearn over and over again.

READING TIME

As you read Chapter 6: "MuscleMemory" in *LeaderFit*, review, reflect on, and respond to the text by answering the following questions.

REVIEW, REFLECT, AND RESPOND:

What are the potential pitfalls of allowing muscle memory, or habit, to determine your approach to leadership, fitness, or life in general?

_____
_____
_____
_____
_____
_____
_____
_____

Have you ever considered that your current ways of thinking could place you in danger of becoming obsolete? How comfortable are you in challenging your norms?

_____
_____
_____
_____
_____
_____
_____
_____

Contemplate the difference between the two statements, "practice makes perfect," and "practice makes permanent." How could this distinction potentially impact your approach to practice, training, or habits you've developed over the years?

_____
_____
_____
_____
_____
_____

Andrew claims Galatians 2:20 as one of his life scriptures. What does it mean to you to be crucified with Christ?

_____
_____
_____
_____
_____
_____

Why do people tend to be resistant to re-learning or re-directing?

_____
_____
_____
_____
_____
_____

What are the most frequent challenges you encounter when it comes to establishing consistent practice of fitness and personal development? What are ways you can begin to overcome these obstacles?

_____
_____
_____
_____

When you find yourself in a particularly busy season, do you find yourself increasingly cutting corners or eliminating things like exercise from your schedule? How can you adjust your approach to stressful times by adopting an attitude more attuned to long-term results over short-term comfort?

_____
_____
_____
_____

Is commonality a desire or temptation for you? Do you find this to be an impediment to achieving your goals?

_____
_____
_____

How can you battle complacency and corrosion in your daily life?

_____
_____
_____

> ## REFLECT ON
>
> *Therefore, I urge you, brothers and sisters, in view of God's mercy, to offer your bodies as a living sacrifice, holy and pleasing to God—this is your true and proper worship. Do not conform to the pattern of this world, but be transformed by the renewing of your mind. Then you will be able to test and approve what God's will is—his good, pleasing and perfect will."*
>
> *—Romans 12:1-2 (NIV)*

Consider Romans 12:1-2, and answer the following questions:

What do you think Paul was trying to convey to the people of Rome when he wrote this letter?

_____
_____
_____
_____
_____
_____
_____

How does the understanding of your body as a living sacrifice impact your willingness to renovate old ways of thinking and living?

_____
_____
_____
_____
_____
_____
_____

What are ways you can purposely seek to place God's will above your own from day to day?

_____
_____
_____
_____
_____
_____
_____

CHAPTER 7

FOLLOW THE LEADER: ARE YOU LEADING OTHERS TO LIFE OR DEATH?

A leader should not be one who only dictates and points out directions or tasks; a true leader is one who knows the way, shows the way, and goes out of their way to ensure that those who are following them become equipped to encounter a new way.

READING TIME

As you read Chapter 7: "Follow the Leader: Are You Leading Others to Life or Death" in *LeaderFit*, review, reflect on, and respond to the text by answering the following questions.

REVIEW, REFLECT, AND RESPOND:

When is the last time you felt the burden of leadership responsibility? What happened and how did you respond?

_____
_____
_____
_____
_____
_____
_____
_____
_____
_____

Have you observed others assume positions of leadership without considering the ramifications? What happened?

_____
_____
_____
_____
_____
_____
_____
_____
_____
_____
_____

If someone seeks your mentorship, what are criteria that you consider before pouring into that individual?

_____
_____
_____
_____
_____

Why is it necessary to remain teachable while in a leadership role?

_____
_____
_____
_____
_____
_____
_____

How aware are you that other people are always watching, listening, and mimicking your words and actions? Does this awareness change, or make you want to change your behaviors or leadership style?

_____
_____
_____
_____
_____
_____
_____
_____

Do you know what you want to model for others? Articulate it now.

_____
_____
_____
_____
_____

Effective leader development involves growth, re-evaluation, and care. How are you integrating these into your personal mentorship approach?

_____
_____
_____
_____
_____

Consider the six levels of leadership development proposed by Dave Ferguson listed on page 94. What are your personal experiences with imparting these to others or having them imparted to you?

_____
_____
_____
_____
_____

Who are the spiritual spotters in your life? Name at least three.

1) _____
2) _____
3) _____

> ## REFLECT ON
>
> *"My dear brothers and sisters, don't be so eager to become a teacher in the church since you know that we who teach are held to a higher standard of judgment."*
>
> —James 3:1 (TPT)

Consider James 3:1, and answer the following questions:

Scripture is clear about teachers in the church being held to a higher standard. How does this correlate to leadership?

_____
_____
_____
_____
_____
_____
_____
_____

What should you consider before seeking positions of leadership?

_____
_____
_____
_____
_____
_____
_____
_____

Have you experienced opportunities to mentor others? Reflect on the experience.

CHAPTER 8

EMOTIONAL FITNESS

Even I needed more than my faith in God when my soul was unexpectedly shipwrecked. I needed the help of God, my counselor, and my spiritual spotters. I also had to choose to rely on spiritual and leadership disciplines developed over time that had become a part of my daily routine. In particular, I had to choose to spend time in prayer and meditation, read the Word of God, get filled by the Word, engage in small group fellowship, and be vulnerable to a few trusted leaders and mentors on my good days and even on my most debilitating days.

READING TIME

As you read Chapter 8: "Emotional Fitness" in *LeaderFit*, review, reflect on, and respond to the text by answering the following questions.

REVIEW, REFLECT, AND RESPOND:

Have you found yourself suppressing past trauma or current internal struggles in order to maintain a certain persona? How is this impacting your mental well-being?

_____
_____
_____
_____
_____
_____
_____
_____
_____
_____
_____

What resources or professionals can you enlist when you find yourself in a mental or emotional crisis?

_____
_____
_____
_____
_____
_____
_____

Andrew shares the pain of the dissolution of his first marriage. Can you relate to such a loss? How did it impact you or how is it impacting you still?

_____
_____
_____
_____
_____

Why is it necessary to understand God as a loving Abba in order to fully invite Him into your emotions?

_____
_____
_____
_____
_____

What was the narrative regarding emotion and feeling that you encountered while growing up? How has this shaped your capacity to acknowledge and express your emotions later in life?

_____
_____
_____
_____
_____
_____
_____
_____
_____

Do you have a directory or source of professionals with whom you can seek personal therapy in times of need? Why might this be a vital component of your community?

_____
_____
_____
_____
_____
_____
_____

Consider the four agreements, as expressed by Don Miguel Ruiz and shared on page 106. How can you incorporate these into your personal coping mechanisms or self-awareness toolbox?

_____
_____
_____
_____
_____

Honestly assess your tendency to play the victim. Is this an area or habit you need to address?

_____
_____
_____
_____
_____

How might you do so?

_____
_____
_____
_____
_____
_____
_____
_____

> **REFLECT ON**
>
> *"Beloved, I pray that you may prosper in all things and be healthy, even as your soul prospers."*
>
> —3 John 1:2 (WEB)

Consider 3 John 1:2, and answer the following questions:

Have you ever considered soul care as integral to your overall wellbeing?

_____
_____
_____
_____
_____
_____
_____
_____

Do you truly believe that God cares for the state of your mind, heart, and body? Are you surrendering all aspects of yourself to Him?

_____
_____
_____
_____
_____
_____
_____
_____

What are ways you can daily entrust God with your physical, spiritual, and emotional well-being?

_____
_____
_____
_____
_____
_____
_____
_____
_____
_____
_____
_____

CHAPTER 9

FAMILY FITNESS

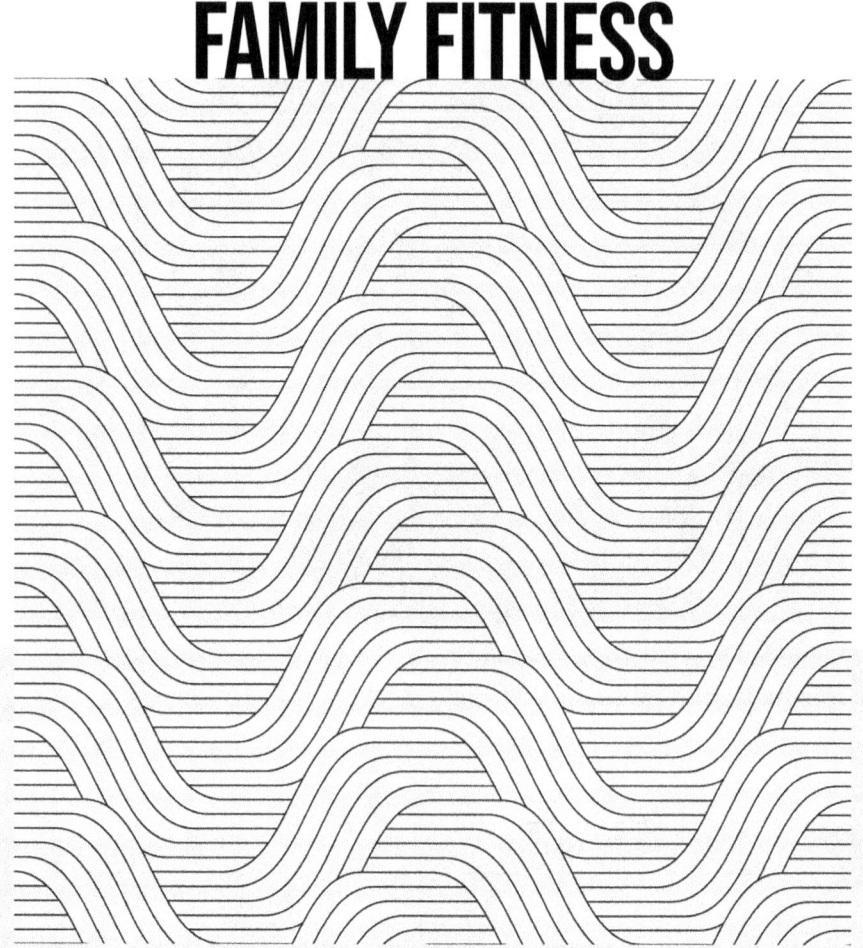

It's not the length or amount of time spent in prayer that has made a difference. It's been the commitment to consistency in prioritizing our family's spiritual wellness and fitness that has been the secret weapon in our intentional time of prayer.

READING TIME

As you read Chapter 9: "Family Fitness" in *LeaderFit*, review, reflect on, and respond to the text by answering the following questions.

REVIEW, REFLECT, AND RESPOND:

What do you think when you hear the phrase, "A family that prays together, stays together"? Does your own family do this regularly? How does it benefit you?

_____
_____
_____
_____
_____
_____
_____
_____
_____

Andrew frequently says, "Remember what I told you in the light when it gets dark." When you encounter dark days, how do you remember what God said about you in lighter times?

_____
_____
_____
_____
_____
_____
_____
_____
_____

What role does honor play in your family relationships?

_____
_____
_____
_____
_____
_____
_____

How does your interpersonal humor and online behavior with your family members reflect the honor to which you esteem them?

_____
_____
_____
_____
_____
_____
_____

Why is mutual respect such a critical component of healthy relationships at home?

_____
_____
_____
_____
_____
_____
_____

How do you maintain trust and transparency at home?

_____
_____
_____
_____
_____

How can you demonstrate mutual generosity within your family?

_____
_____
_____
_____
_____
_____
_____
_____

What are your core family values? Identify at least four.

1) _____

2) _____

3) _____

4) _____

> ## REFLECT ON
> *There is a time for everything and a season for every activity under the heavens; a time to plant and a time to uproot, a time to kill and a time to heal, a time to tear down and a time to build, a time to weep and a time to laugh, a time to mourn and a time to dance, a time to scatter stones and a time to gather them, a time to embrace and a time to refrain from embracing, a time to search and a time to give up, a time to keep and a time to throw away, a time to tear and a time to mend, a time to be silent and a time to speak, a time to love and a time to hate, a time for war and a time for peace.*
>
> —*Ecclesiastes 3:1-8 (NIV)*

Consider Ecclesiastes 3:1-8 and answer the following questions:

Are you aware that marriage and family life have different seasons? Are you loving towards your spouse in this season the same as you were two years ago?

_____
_____
_____
_____
_____

What are various causes of season change?

_____
_____
_____
_____
_____

What does it mean to have grace towards your spouse as you weather different seasons of life together?

_____
_____
_____
_____
_____
_____
_____

CHAPTER 10

LEADERFIT UNLEASHED

*To be fit is to live a purposeful life with
gratitude, joy, and wholeness.*

READING TIME

As you read Chapter 10: "LeaderFit Unleashed" in *LeaderFit*, review, reflect on, and respond to the text by answering the following questions.

REVIEW, REFLECT, AND RESPOND:

Andrew motivates others by saying, "There's another you in you!" Are you able to recognize and unearth your inner potential? How will you do so today?

_____
_____
_____
_____
_____
_____
_____
_____
_____

Are you satisfied with the way you are currently existing? Why or why not?

_____
_____
_____
_____
_____
_____
_____
_____
_____
_____
_____

How can you unleash the dormant qualities that reside within you?

Where has delay been an enemy of progress in your life?

What are you willing to risk to uncover and become the best version of yourself?

Why is a commitment to finishing critical to your personal success?

What is the role fitness can play in your role as a leader?

___

How can physical fitness improve your life?

___

Reconsider the definition of LeaderFit previously laid out in the text. "LeaderFit is the conditioned ability to positively influence, motivate, equip, and empower others to the achievement of a goal or outcome over a sustained period of time with sustaining impact." How has your understanding of this concept evolved? Once more, ask yourself, are you LeaderFit?

___

> **REFLECT ON**
> *Give us today our daily bread.*
>
> *—Matthew 6:11 (NIV)*

Consider Matthew 6:11, and answer the following questions:

Why do you think the Bible prompts us to ask God only for what we need today?

___

How does the notion of "die empty daily" correlate with this verse?

___

How can you apply this concept to your daily life?

___

www.ingramcontent.com/pod-product-compliance
Lightning Source LLC
Chambersburg PA
CBHW070208100426
42743CB00013B/3104